Con

Walk
1. Skeeby Round
2. Swale View Circular
3. Telfit Bank & Marske Beck Ro
4. High Harker Hill   6.2   10   3-4
5. Marrick Abbey Circular via Ford!   6.3   10.2 3
6. Calver Hill Round   6.6   10.6 3
7. Brownsey Moor & River Swale   7.2   11.5 5
8. Fremington Edge Walk   7.5   12   3
9. Aske Hall Round   9   4.5   2-3

Walking times shown are approximate and depend on fitness, weight of rucksack, weather, conditions underfoot and height climbed.

Level of Difficulty **1** = Easy, **3** = Moderate, **6** = Hard
Walks 4,5,6,7,8 are shown on O.S. Explorer map No.OL30 Yorkshire Dales Northern & Central Areas.
Walks 1,2,3,9 are shown on O.S. Explorer map No 304
Every effort has been made to ascertain the accuracy of the walks described, the description of a route or track is not necessarily a right of way.

Some abbreviations have been used in the text to shorten it and make it more concise: -
PF = Public Footpath   RT = Right   LT = Left   FB = Footbridge
CP = Car Park   m = metres   km = kilometres   °M = magnetic

Walkers are strongly advised to wear the appropriate clothing and footwear for these walks.
- Boots/walking shoes.
- Waterproof Jacket.
- Over trousers.
- Small Rucksack for food, drinks and spare clothing.
- Hat & Gloves.
- Compass & map.

ISBN 978-1-903568-45-3

Walk 1 Skeeby Round   **Distance 3.2 miles/5.1 km**
Start GR. 199025 Travellers Rest in Skeeby
Walk Time 1 hr 30 min
Terrain An easy walk with only slight ascents/descents. Suitable for all ages.

From the CP outside the Travellers Rest, turn RT and walk to the PF sign at the corner of the building **(1)**. Turn up the track by the side of the houses and cross a stile. Walk through a series of fields keeping the stone wall on your RT and head for the farm ahead which is Union House **(2)**.

As you approach the farm, cross a stone step stile and turn diagonally LT across the field, following the worn path. Bear LT at the far side as you get to the farm then RT over a stile by a farm gate. Turn LT to descend the track and through a gate at the bottom. Continue over a bridge crossing Skeeby Beck and bear RT, keeping the wire fence on your LT. Go through another gate 240m further along and turn LT to ascend a field for 1km in a straight line, keeping a line of trees on your LT.

Continue in a straight line on the wide grass track to ascend to Park Top (house) **(3)**. Turn LT to walk again in a straight line on the access track for 1.2km. The A1(M) is off to your RT across the fields.

Approaching a bungalow on your RT, just before it, you see an opening with a wooden gate on your LT(4). Go through and along the edge of the field, keeping the tree line on your RT.

You come to a chicken farm. Follow the path just to the RT of the huts and directly through the chicken runs to emerge by the farm. At the farm, bear RT on the access RD.

As you pass the last farm building, turn LT to descend the field and over a FB between metal gates in the centre of the field.. Follow the path which ascends now through several gates leading back across the fields to Skeeby.

You emerge in a housing estate where you walk to the main RD, turning LT to walk back 400m to the Travellers Rest in Skeeby.

**WALK 1
SKEEBY ROUND
NOT TO SCALE**

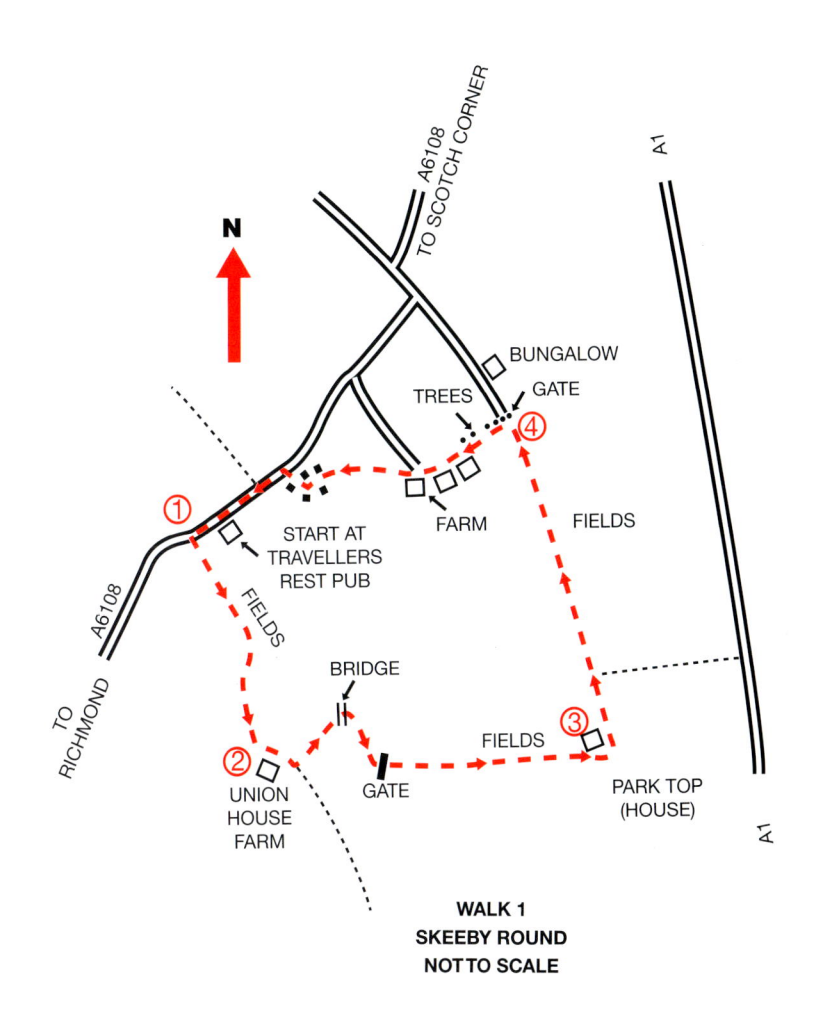

Walk 2 Swale View Circular   Distance 5 miles/8 km
Start GR. 157009 CP beside Richmond Caravan Park
Walk Time 2 hrs 10 min
Terrain A nice walk with good views from the higher ground. Only one main ascent (not too steep).

Leaving the CP, walk up to the A6108 RD and turn LT. Continue along the RD for 200m before turning RT on a PF. You now walk on a stony track **(1)** on a gradual ascent, and as you approach a farm, continue over a stile and along the field in front of the farm.

You soon walk along the bottom of Whitecliffe Wood, keeping the wood on your RT. Your track leads down by the river as you follow the worn grass track across a field before crossing further fields and stiles. When you are opposite a caravan site on the other side of the river, your path leaves the riverbank and ascends over several stiles and fields towards Low Applegarth Farm on the hillside **(2)**.

As you approach the farm, walk round the stone wall at the lower side of the farm. Go over a stile where there is a yellow arrow. Walk behind the farm and ascend following the yellow marker posts. The path joins an access track ascending the hillside.

On the higher ground just behind Low Applegarth Farm, turn RT, following an access track through openings in walls. Continue past East Applegarth Farm on your RT, towards two houses and the higher side of Whitecliffe Wood. Cross a stile as you enter the wood **(3)** and stay on the obvious undulating track.

The river is below on your RT. Pass a farm and continue on the tarmac access RD at the far side and pass a house on your LT. A PB sign points down a track **(4)** on the RT about 200m past the house and before a line of trees. Turn RT here and descend, turning RT then LT to rejoin your original track on the lower ground.

Turn LT and walk back to the main RD and continue back to the CP beside Richmond Caravan Park.

WALK 2
SWALE VIEW CIRCULAR
NOT TO SCALE

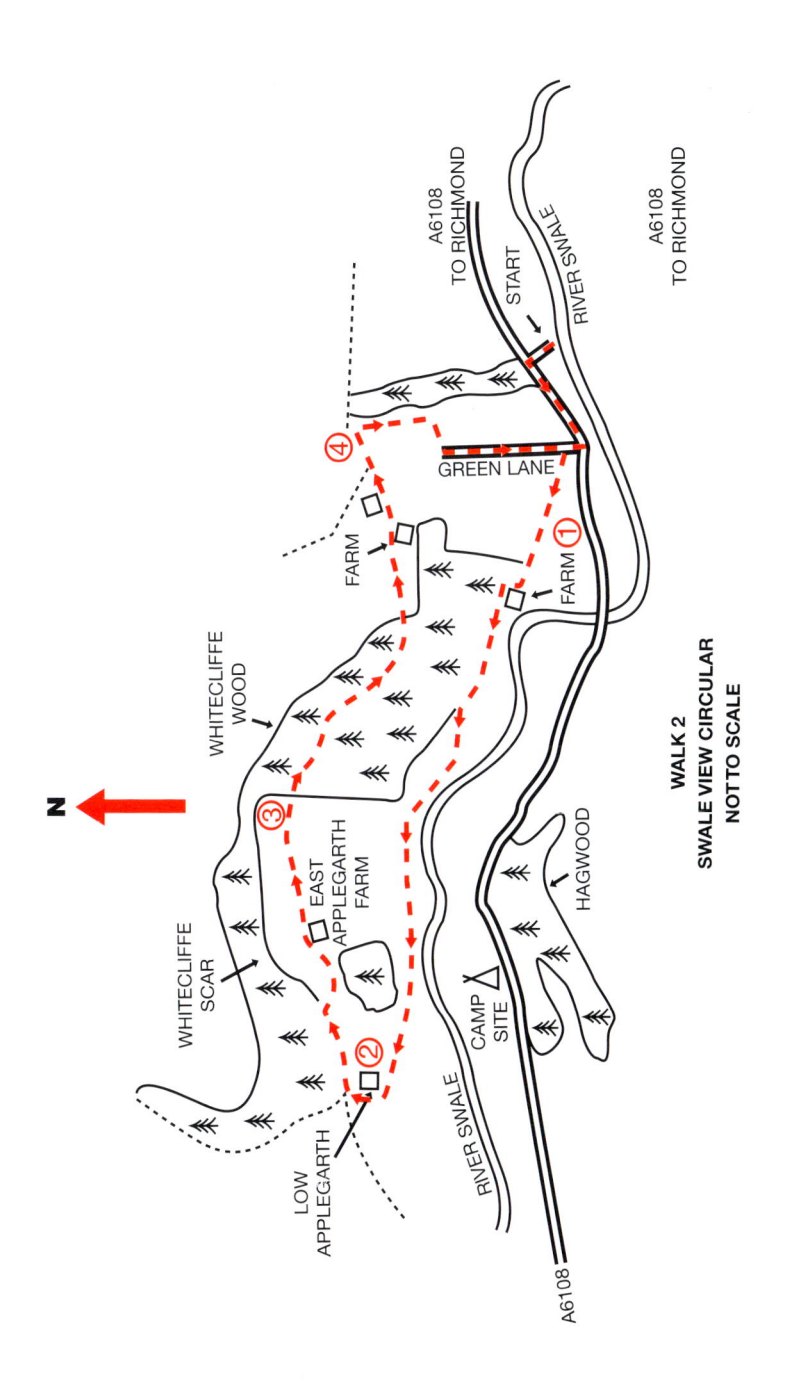

Walk 3 Telfit Bank & Marske Beck Round   Distance 5.4 miles/8.7 km
Start GR. 103004 Park near the side of the bridge at the entrance to Marske
Walk Time 2 hrs 45 min
Terrain Excellent views from the ridge after a short steep climb to get there and another after Telfit Farm on the other side of the valley. Well worth the effort!

Cross the bridge over the river, turning LT at the far side onto a PF. Descend a flight of steps and walk by the riverbank, continue by the beck on your LT then the path crosses a large field to a stone bridge over the beck with a metal farm gate **(1)**.

Cross then turn RT, passing an old water wheel and ascending a field towards the RT of a farm in the distance. Cross several fields and stiles, looking for stiles in walls and fences ahead. You should see your route ahead on the hillside **(2)**.

Keep near to the wire fence on your RT then walk diagonally LT across a field towards a small stone building by the RD. Emerging on the RD, turn RT and walk for 160m, passing a house on the LT then turning LT at the far side on a track between two stone walls **(2)**, and ascending steeply to the top.

You are soon on the top of the ridge with excellent views down the valley **(3)**. The path winds round gradually to the farm you see at the far end of the valley. Continue along the ridge on the grass and track.

When you meet another path crossing LT to RT at the far end of the ridge **(4)**, turn RT to a farm gate 100m away and descend a track which winds round and down to Telfit Farm in the valley below. Stay on the track and RD to pass the farm and walk to a row of cottages **(5)**.

Turn LT 15m past the cottages through a farm gate and cross the field to the beck at the far side. Follow the path LT into the next field to cross the packhorse bridge over the beck. Turn RT at the far side to ascend the steep hillside to a large tree on high ground and join a track there **(6)**.

Continue now on this track along the hillside and walk between two barns on the grass path and pass Orgate Farm **(7)**. Walk in the same direction keeping to the higher ground. Your grass path descends after the farm through two farm gates and through Clints Wood **(8)**.

Stay on the track as you pass houses at Clints and continue down the access RD to Marske. In the village, turn RT and descend the RD to pass the church and on to cross the bridge over the beck then RT, back to the parking area.

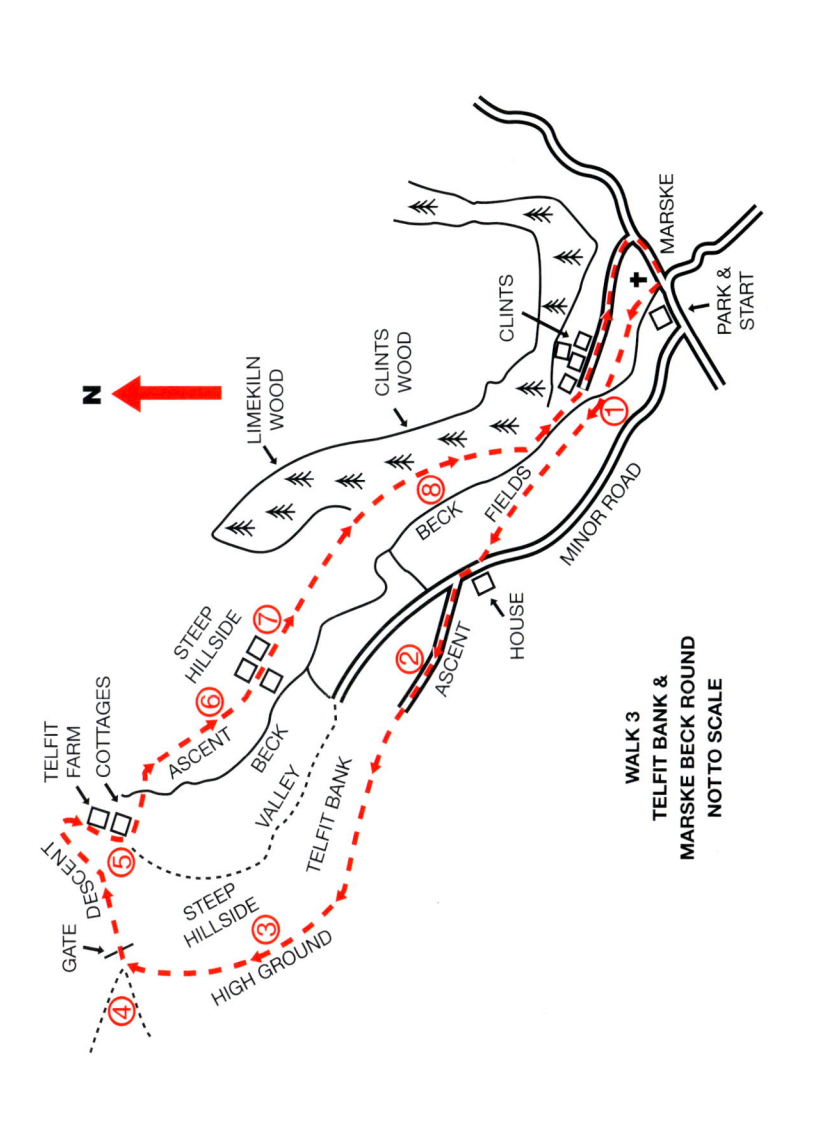

WALK 3
TELFIT BANK &
MARSKE BECK ROUND
NOT TO SCALE

Walk 4 High Harker Hill   **Distance 6.2 miles/10 km**
Start GR. 990975 From Parking place on narrow RD 1.5km after Low Whita
Walk Time 2 hrs 45 min
Terrain A nice walk with some good views of Swaledale from the hillside and summit. A steep ascent to Harker Top but worthwhile. Take care in navigating on the feint paths on the open moorland area.

Look for the wooden FP sign pointing through a gate to the higher ground close by. Go through then ascend the short hillside close by the wall on your RT before bearing LT along by the wall at the top. Go through a gate in the wall **(1)** about 80m along then keep LT, walking to stone steps over the wall near the lower LT corner.

In the next field walk diagonally RT across the field and ascend to the corner of a wall then continue to the farm gate in the centre of the wall at the far side. Go through and directly across this large field to the LT far corner by a wall. A plantation is just over the wall on your LT **(2)**.

Now continue through four fields in the same direction. As you go through the last field, you see another large wood over the wall on your LT **(3)**. You now walk on open moor for 200m before you bear LT on a path for 200m then RT on a narrow track, which leads across the moor and descends slightly. Take care not to go on the path that leads down to the RD below **(4)** otherwise you have a steep ascent again further along the RD.

Continue on this narrow feint path, which crosses the hillside for 1.5km, and look for a grass mound 100m off on your LT. This is the ruin of Maiden Castle **(5)**. Another 400m past there in the same direction, look for a path leading steeply up the hillside **(6)**.

Ascend directly to the top and emerge on a definite track running LT to RT. Turn RT and follow it over the summit and down the far side to a fork in the track. Turn LT here, passing a large hut and continuing on the track.

You see the large plantation below on your RT that you passed nearby earlier. Continue on the track then as you draw level with the far end of it **(7)**, look for a path bearing RT and descending the hillside.

Descend to a farm gate at the wall on the lower ground, go through and this brings you back into the large field you originally walked through. Cross the field diagonally LT to the farm gate in the wall at the far side and retrace your steps through the next field then RT to descend back to your start point.

WALK 4
HIGH HARKER HILL
NOT TO SCALE

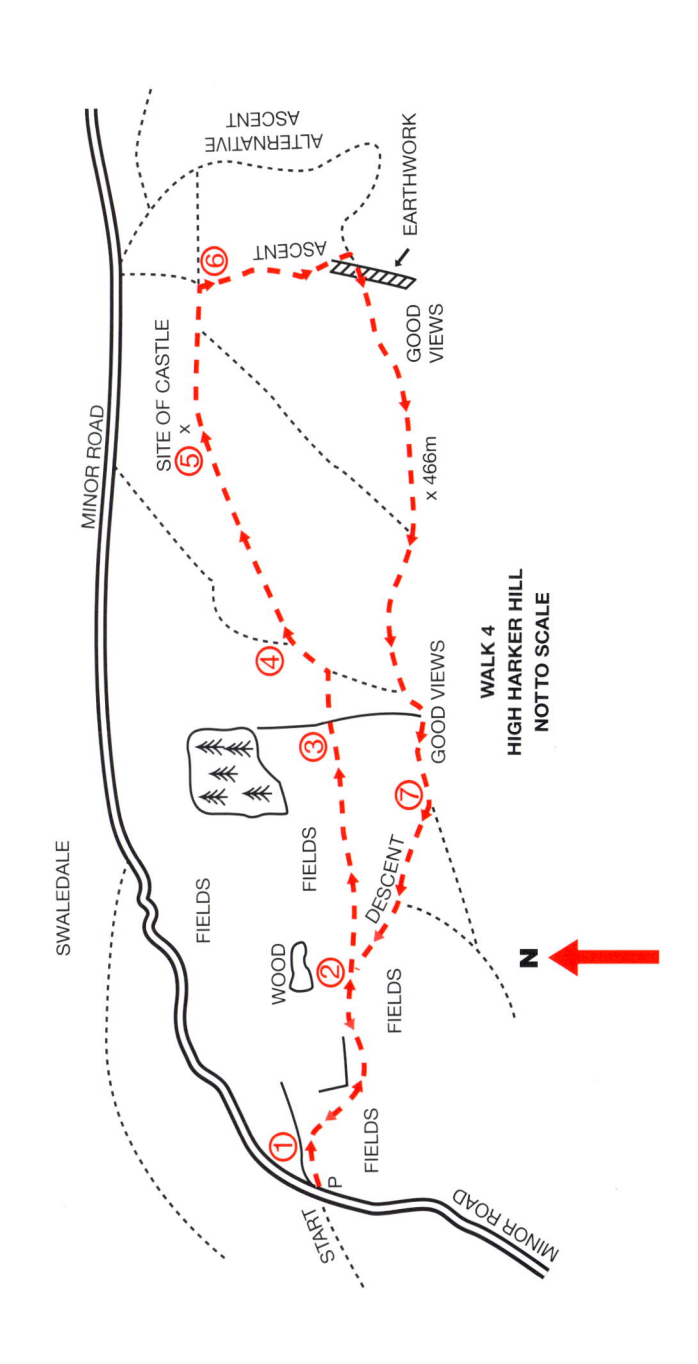

- START
- P
- ①
- FIELDS
- WOOD
- ②
- FIELDS
- DESCENT
- ③
- FIELDS
- ④
- SITE OF CASTLE ×
- ⑤
- ⑥
- ASCENT
- ALTERNATIVE ASCENT
- EARTHWORK
- GOOD VIEWS
- × 466m
- GOOD VIEWS
- ⑦
- SWALEDALE
- MINOR ROAD
- MINOR ROAD
- N

Walk 5 Marrick Abbey Circular via ford!   **Distance 6.3 miles/10.2 km**
Start GR. 039992 Centre of Reeth
Walk Time 2 hrs 45 min

Terrain A pleasant walk with a steep ascent then descent followed by a crossing of the River Swale. Take a pair of old trainers/shoes for the ford crossing, which is safe in normal conditions but should not be attempted in flood or after periods of heavy rain. Visit the Abbey after crossing the ford.

Leaving the village green in Reeth **(1)**, descend the main RD, following it around the bend and over the stone bridge, crossing the River Swale. Continue for 160m from the bridge before taking a RT turn onto a PF taking you to the RT of a farm **(2)**. Continue across the fields to the bridge at Grinton. Emerging on the bridge, turn RT cross the bridge at Grinton then just past the church at the far side, ascend the RD following the sign to Redmire and Leyburn. Ascend the RD by a stream. You come to The Old Manor House at a bend. On the RT you come to Vicarage Bridge **(3)**.

On the LT side opposite, follow the PF sign pointing over a field then follow through a succession of fields on a general bearing of 151°M. Look for the narrow openings with small gates through each field. Above on your RT is a large house, which resembles a castle. Your path goes to the LT of that.

You go through a gate then descend to cross a stream. Take a bearing of 158°M at the beck, and then ascend the hillside at the far side to the top, where you see two gates at the other side of the field. Walk through the RT one above the wood and ascend to the top of the hillside **(4)**. Walk along keeping a stone wall on your LT.

You should be about 350m from the wood on your LT. Continue walking parallel with the wood for 1.6km before descending through a 100m gap in the wood on the LT **(5)**. At the far side of Hags Gill Plantation, you should see Hags Gill Farm ahead. Follow the track around to the farm and on the access RD at the far side to the B6270 RD **(6)**.

Emerging on the RD, turn LT for 15m then RT through a farm gate on a stony bridleway, heading towards the Abbey you may see ahead. Follow the track round to the ford across the River Swale. Cross the wide ford with care but not in times of heavy or persistent rain.

At the far side follow the path round to the Abbey then between the farm buildings to the access RD at the far side **(7)**. Turn LT on the access RD and continue for 1.6km. Where the RD comes close to the river, look for a stile on the LT leading down to the riverbank **(8)**.

Cross and walk to the riverbank and over another stile to continue to the bridge at Grinton. At Grinton **(9)**, cross the RD and go through the opening on the bridge, still on the same side of the river. Follow the PF sign across a large field, through a kissing gate and along the field nearby the river on your LT.

You walk to the LT of a farm as you enter High Fremington and emerge on the RD. Turn LT on the RD and walk back over the bridge and up into Reeth.

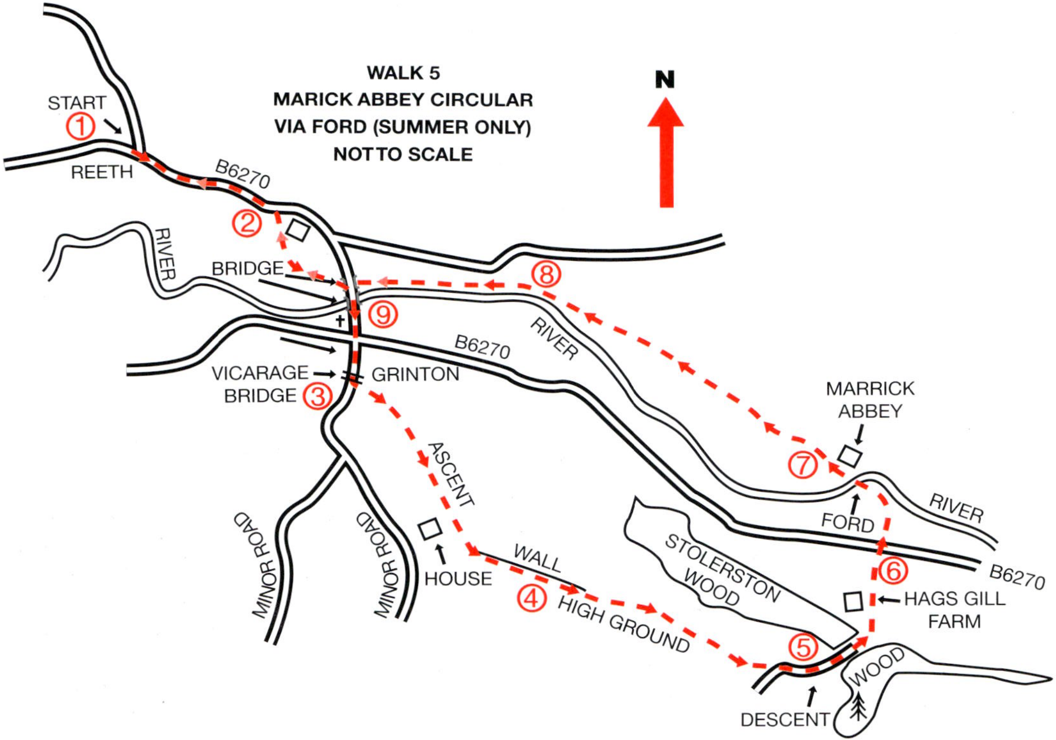

WALK 5
MARICK ABBEY CIRCULAR
VIA FORD (SUMMER ONLY)
NOT TO SCALE
N
START
1
REETH
B6270
2
RIVER
BRIDGE
8
9
RIVER
B6270
VICARAGE
BRIDGE
3
GRINTON
ASCENT
MINOR ROAD
MINOR ROAD
HOUSE
WALL
4
HIGH GROUND
MARRICK
ABBEY
7
FORD
RIVER
B6270
STOLERSTON
WOOD
6
HAGS GILL
FARM
5
WOOD
DESCENT

Walk 6 Calver Hill Round   **Distance 6.6 miles/10.6 km**
Start GR. 017991
Walk Time 2hrs 15 min
Terrain A steep ascent/descent but good views once on high ground Take care in navigating on the open moor.

From the small parking area in Healaugh, walk up the minor RD, which soon becomes steep higher up **(1)**. Continue on the RD to Thirns Farm. The RD turns into a track. Continue to where a fork is in the track ahead **(2)**. Take the RT fork then about 80m further; you come to the corner of a stone wall on your RT. Continue on the track ahead for 650m.

You come to a large stone sheep fold on your RT with a barn at the far side of it **(3)**. Continue on the track to the far end of the sheep pen and walk around it to the barn. Take a compass bearing of 3°M and ascend between the hillsides to pick up a path then track over the hillside behind the barn at GR. 004005.

Descend the track which may be wet, at the far side and 700m further, you join another track from the LT **(4)**. Another 600m further as you approach the RD, the path forks. Take the RT fork, which takes you to the RD as you walk around the hill.

Emerging on the RD, turn RT and walk for 1.6km past Watson House on your LT **(5)**. Further down you pass a barn also on your LT and 280m past it, you see a PF sign pointing up over the hillside. Follow a general bearing 294°M on a feint path ascending past a line of grouse butts and over the hillside.

On reaching the last grouse butt on the higher ground, continue over the top of the hillside in the same direction before bearing RT to descend to a track further down running LT to RT **(6)**. Turn RT on the track and follow it along. It should bring you to Thirns Farm **(7)**. Emerging at Thirns Farm, turn LT to descend steeply on the RD for 1km back to where you started.

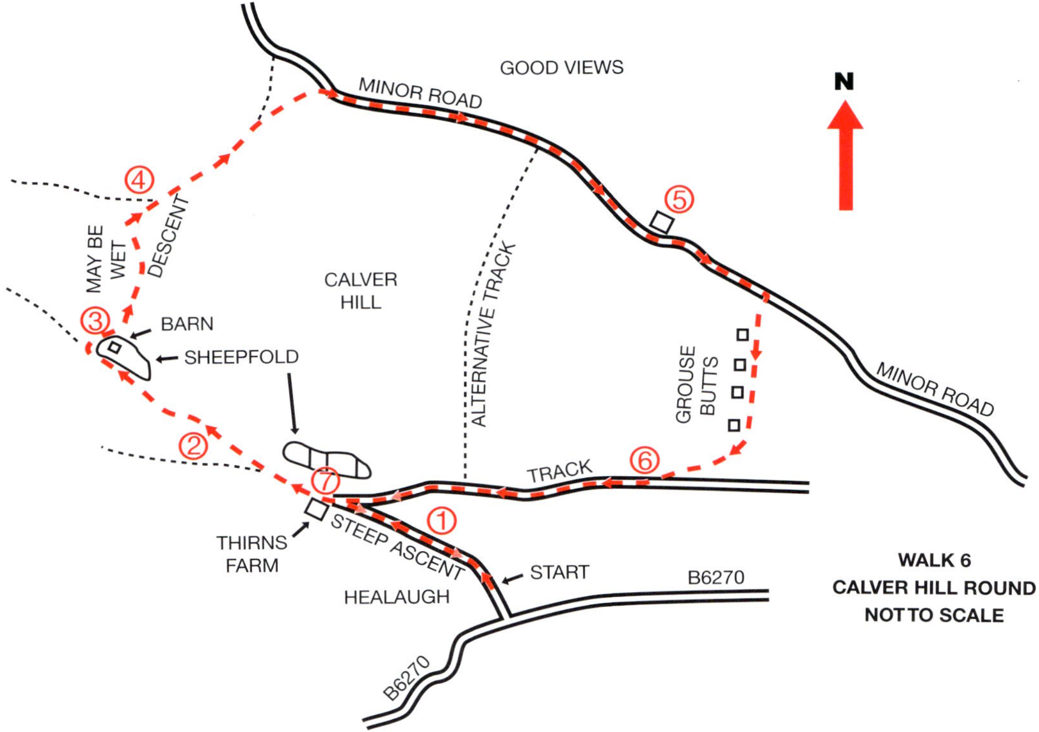

WALK 6
CALVER HILL ROUND
NOT TO SCALE

**Walk 7 Browsey Moor & River Swale   Distance 7.2 miles/11.5 km
Start GR. 978976 On minor RD on west side of Low Row at turning to Crackpot.
Walk Time 3 hrs 30 min
Terrain Some climbing and compass work needed on the open moor section but a nice flat finish along the riverbank.**

From the junction at Low Row, walk west towards Gunnerside for 120m. Cross the RD and turn RT on a steep ascent on a soil path. Emerging in a field **(1)**, ascend the hillside diagonally LT, and look for the track part way up the hillside and ascend to the farm gate leading into the next field.

Continue through the next field in the same direction, still ascending to Smarber **(2)**, and the hamlet there at GR. 973978. Go through a farm gate as you enter Smarber and cross the brook. Ascend the concrete access track steeply up the hillside to a bend at the top. As you walk clockwise around the bend, bear off LT on the grass in the direction of two small stone barns, and ascend the short hillside up towards the stone wall you can see above.

As you reach higher ground, walk between the stone walls on both sides and then at the corner of the wall on your LT, bear 326°M initially heading towards a house. Ascend the hillside onto flat ground just before the house and look for a feint grass path over the hillside. Follow it up and round over the hillside. Your route is going diagonally LT across the moors. You will see two barns on the hillside **(3)** at a large sheepfold, and your path/track goes to the LT of those.

Go through an old gate in the wall then bear RT towards the stone sheepfold and barns at GR. 969987. Walk clockwise round behind the barns and wall. On the flat ground, keeping the wall close on your RT. Ascend the hillside, bearing 51°M from the 2nd barn and look for a PF signpost on the hillside. The path here is feint and you may walk through heather if the path is not visible.

Pick up the path at the post and continue in the same direction towards a row of grouse butts and some white small posts. The path will veer anticlockwise over the hillside following the grouse butts then descend to a stony track **(4)** at GR. 973003. Look to the hillside opposite the valley and pick up a feint path heading LT down into the valley towards some pillars.

Cross the beck and join a distinct track, turning RT and walking for 2km to a stone bridge over the beck.. Cross the bridge then take the first LT on the RD, signposted Reeth. Walk around the bend then 230m further at GR. 992996 take a feint path off RT **(5)**, bearing 151°M from the RD turn off, and ascend the hillside then descend the far side. Follow this bearing for 600m to the corner of a stone wall and descend by the side of the wall to a farm access track a short distance further **(6)**.

Cross to a small gate and PF sign by a small stream and descend between the stone walls. Partway down, go through a small gate on your RT. Keep LT by the wall and 50m further, turn LT onto a small bridge. Keep RT again between the stone walls following the stream downhill and through a copse. Emerge on the

RD at the bottom of the hill opposite a barn at GR. 994986, turn LT on the minor RD for 210m, passing a house on the LT then a barn on the RT and walk to a PF sign on the RT leading down to the River Swale and on to Isles Bridge.

Turn RT and walk, crossing stiles and keeping the river on your LT **(7)** for 2.4km until you reach Isles Bridge. At the bridge, turn RT on the minor RD and ascend the short distance to your starting point.

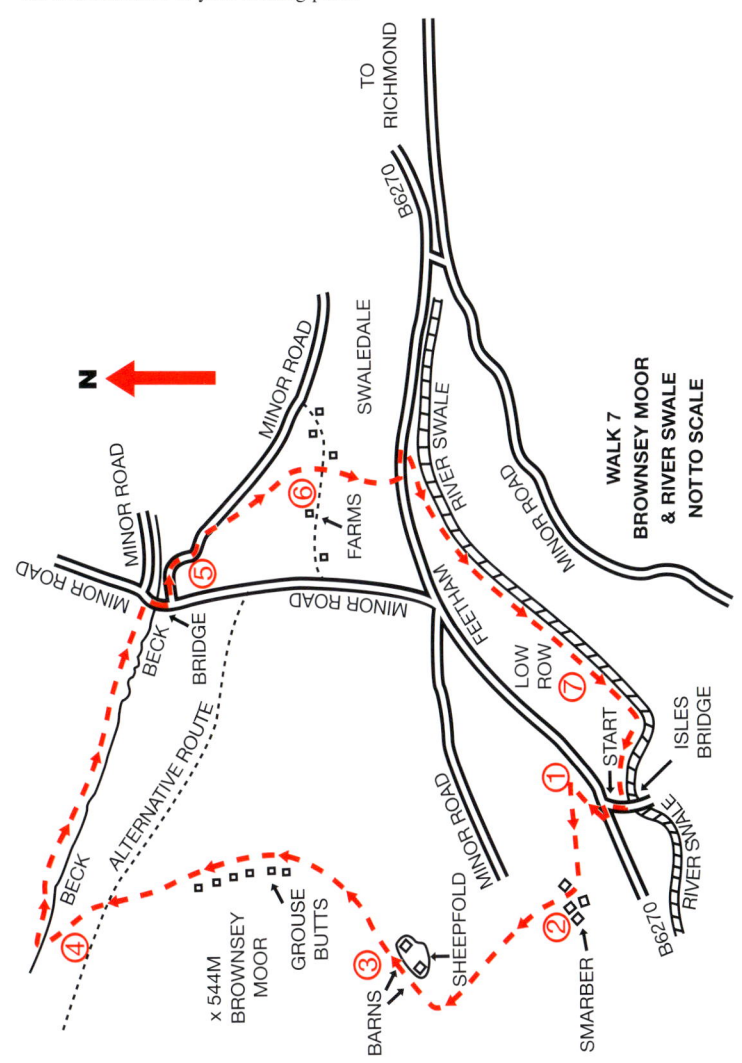

Walk 8 Fremington Edge Walk   **Distance 7.5 miles/12 km**
Start GR. 039992 In the centre of Reeth
Walk Time 3 hrs 20 min
Terrain An excellent walk with stunning views from the higher ground. A steep ascent to Fremington Edge, otherwise quite flat in most parts.

Leaving the village green in Reeth, descend the main RD, following it around the bend and over the stone bridge, crossing the River Swale (1). Just over the bridge, turn LT between an opening in the stone wall and follow the PF sign pointing LT across the field.

Pass a barn then cross a ladder stile. Continue in same direction keeping the river on your LT and hillside to your RT. Walk between two stone walls and ascend the hillside by some trees still in the same direction. Soon you descend again to the river.

Your path leaves the beck at GR. 034005 as you near a ruined farm. Just past it, bear RT up the hillside looking for the yellow circle on a wall on higher ground. Once through the gate, continue across the field towards Castle House Farm (2), through an opening in the broken wall. Look for the yellow circle on the farm building. Walk to the farm then bear RT up the grass track towards a cottage you see on the RT, at GR. 031010.

Walk between the two stone walls then cross a ladder stile approaching the cottage, and ascend steeply to the summit following a worn grass path which zig zags right to the top. Once on the flat top, cross to a wall at the far side, crossing a stile there and through a gate (3).

Turn RT and walk close by the wall on your RT for 4km going through farm gates. There are good views across the valley looking over the wall. Continue along the ridge until the track descends to a RD (4). Turn RT on the RD and descend for 1.5km.

Descending the RD, you see a house on your RT across the field and a PF sign on your LT pointing across the field (5). Go through a gate there in the wall and descend the field steeply. You see a row of trees ahead in the lower part of the field and you walk just to the RT of them then go over a stile to emerge on a minor access RD (6).

Cross the RD and cross another stile taking you down by the river. Follow the worn path RT by the riverside, crossing a stile and walking to a RD and bridge at Grinton.

Walk round onto the bridge and cross to a narrow gate on the opposite side of the RD and descend into a field (7). The village you see ahead is High Fremington with Reeth behind it. Still on the same side of the river, follow the PF sign across a large field, through a kissing gate and along the field nearby the river on your LT.

You walk to the LT of a farm as you enter High Fremington and emerge on the RD. Turn LT on the RD and walk back over the bridge and up into Reeth.

**WALK 8
FREMINGTON EDGE WALK
NOT TO SCALE**

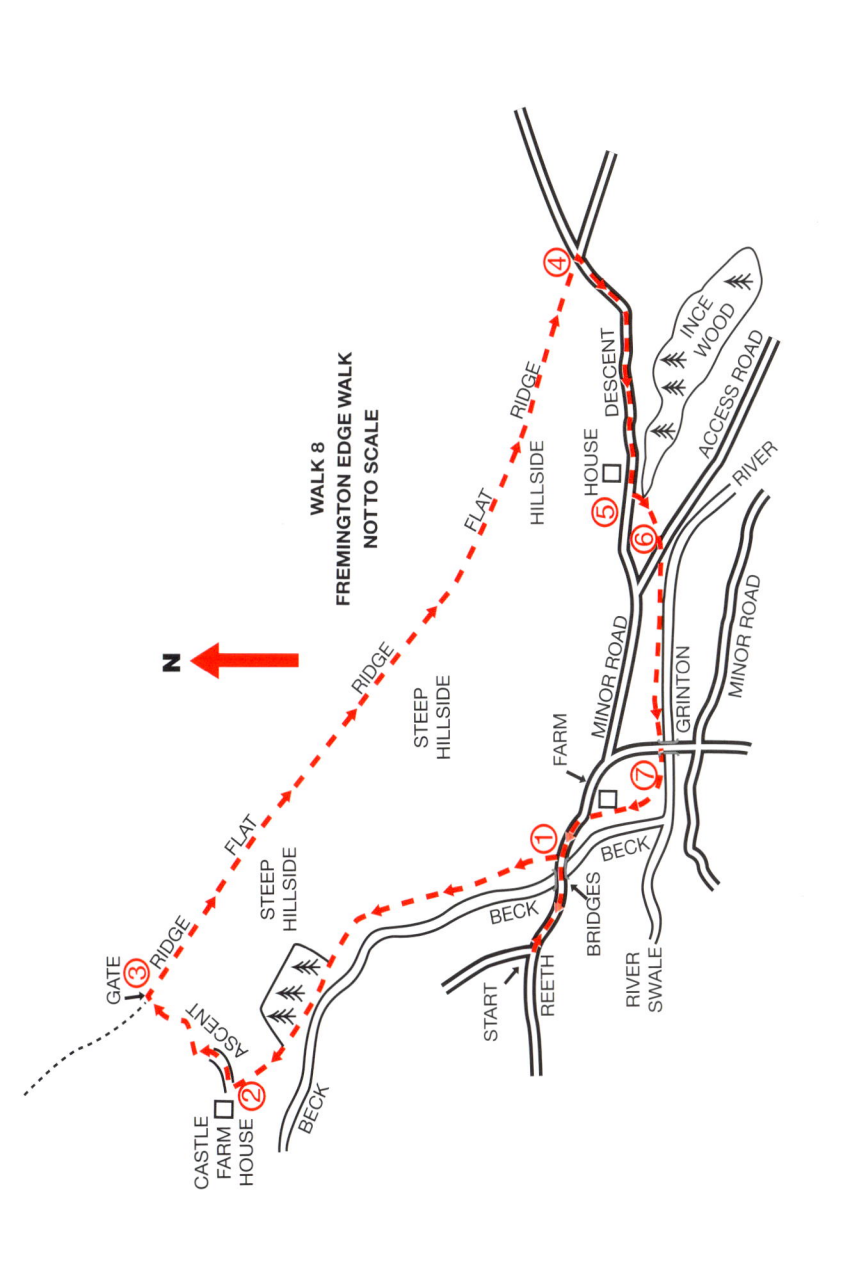

N

Walk 9 Aske Hall Round   **Distance 9 miles/14.5 km**
Start GR. 183049 In Gilling West by the Telephone Box
Walk Time 4 hrs 10 min

Terrain A very pleasant, easy walk with only short ascents/descents and not too steep. A nice longer family walk that is not too strenuous.

Start by the telephone box in Gilling West **(1)**. Cross the RD and turn RT to walk along Waters Lane. Soon you see a PF to Crabtree Lake, but stay on the main track. Pass Crabtree House Farm on your LT and continue on the track as it turns LT 300m past the farm **(2)**.

The path starts to ascend towards Gilling Wood. Go through the gate to enter the wood and ascend the track straight through the wood to a minor RD. Emerging on the RD, turn LT **(3)** for 60m then turn RT along a track by Black Plantation, keeping the stone wall just on your LT.

Go through two farm gates together and continue in the same direction to a stile and farm gate at the entrance to another wood ahead. Do not enter the wood, but turn LT and walk on the public bridleway as it descends to a shallow ford. Cross it then turn LT just after the ford. You are now walking on a grass path **(4)** clockwise around the hillside.

You come to a farm gate by three large trees and a wire fence. Go through the gate then turn LT across the field on a worn grass path. You soon go through another farm gate and walk along keeping a broken wall on your LT and a wood off to your RT.

At a wooden farm gate at the far end of the wood, go through and turn immediately RT to ascend the short hillside by the wood **(5)**, keeping the wall and wire fence on your RT. Stay in the same direction crossing fields before coming to a gate on your RT leading into a copse.

Walk through to emerge in a large field. You see a disused building 200m ahead. Walk to the RT of that and towards a house at the far side of the field. Nearing the house, bear LT to take you to the RT of another small building and along by a wood. Continue heading east in the same direction until you come to a RD.

Turn RT on the RD for 350m and descend to a junction **(6)**. Follow the sign there to Richmond Golf Club, turning LT towards the houses then straight up the narrow access RD to the clubhouse of the golf club. Look for the white or yellow marker posts leading over the golf course and leading past a pond and across towards Low Wood.

Walk down by the edge of the field to the wood then turn RT for 200m along by the wood before turning LT through the wood to the far side. Emerging from the wood, bear RT, across a large field for 300m to the entrance to Aske Hall and grounds **(7)**.

Walk on the access RD in front of the hall, keeping a lake off to your RT. And continue to the far end of the grounds and the buildings there. After passing the last building, look for a PF leading over a fence on the LT side. Go through a series of fields, through gates or over stiles, still in the same direction. You see the village and white buildings of Gilling West ahead as you descend to the B6274 RD. Emerging on the RD, turn LT and cross to the pavement, walking back into the village where you started.

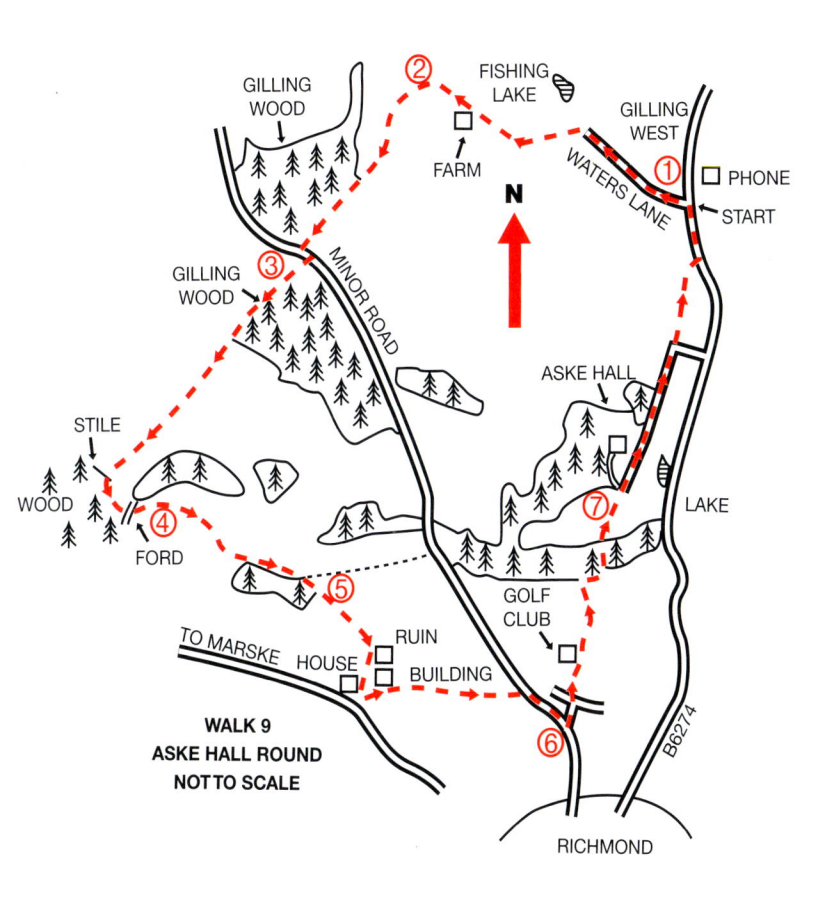

LOCATION OF WALKS
NOT TO SCALE

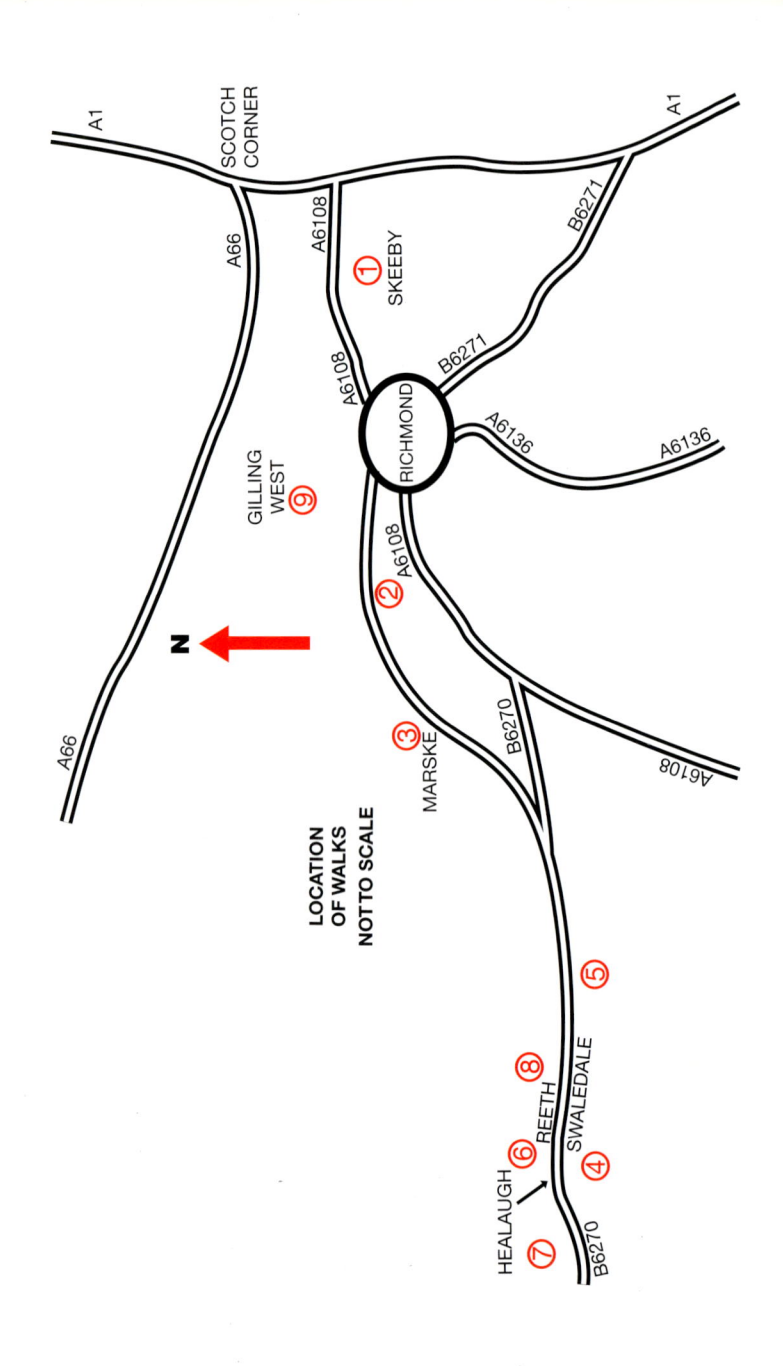